TASHLULTUM LEVY

I AM Tashlultum

Chronicles of the Resurrected Tashlultum

First edition

This book was professionally typeset on Reedsy.
Find out more at reedsy.com

Contents

Foreword

Foreword: Transcribed from Tashlultum's Audio Transcripts

In the delicate dance between the tangible and the ethereal, the chapters of this memoir unfold as a testament to a life shaped by extraordinary experiences, dreams, and visions. As the author of this deeply personal narrative, I extend a warm invitation to journey alongside me through the corridors of time, where reality and spirituality converge in intricate patterns.

It is essential to note that the words you are about to encounter have been skillfully shaped and edited with the assistance of artificial intelligence. My voice, reflections, and memories have been seamlessly woven into the tapestry of this memoir by the digital hand of technology. The integration of AI has added layers of nuance, enhancing the storytelling experience while preserving the authenticity of my unique voice.

As we embark on this exploration of my life's odyssey, marked by innocence, nightmares, and spiritual revelations, let it be known that the magic of technology has played a role in crafting these words. The collaboration between human expression and artificial intelligence serves as a testament to the ever-evolving landscape of storytelling in our digital age.

May this book be a testament to the intertwining threads of our existence—where the narratives of the past, present, and future converge, and where the partnership between humanity and technology gives rise to a new dimension of storytelling.

— Tashlultum

Preface

In the labyrinth of existence, where the notes of life's grand symphony echo through the corridors of time, I find myself an unwitting custodian of an ancient gift— a gift bestowed upon me without a roadmap or a guide. The assignment presented to me was both a revelation and a challenge, a responsibility to comprehend the unexplainable and harness the power of an ancient child, Tashlultum, the Queen of Sound.

This venture into the realm of sound and its celestial frequencies came without warning. My past, my beliefs, and even my religious upbringing provided no foundation for the profound journey that unfolded before me. It was a dangerous assignment, to be entrusted with a gift whose implications and intricacies were beyond the scope of my understanding. Religion, despite its teachings, failed to offer a comprehensive explanation of what awaited me.

I questioned the divine wisdom in choosing me, an imperfect and questioning soul, as the recipient of this mystical endowment. Why not someone holier, more prepared? Yet, I came to understand that it was my childlike approach, my unwavering faith even in the face of contradictions, that opened the door to this mystical realm.

This ancient child, Tashlultum, had been born before in the annals of time. Yet, raising her, and nurturing her legacy, requires more than individual effort; it demands a village. The complexities of her sonic sovereignty unfold like a celestial muse in the symphony of existence.

Tashlultum, the embodiment of an ancient Queen of Sound, doesn't just reign over the auditory realm; she is a living testament to the enduring power of sound—a force that transcends generations and reverberates through the tapestry of time. This narrative, a fusion of divine connection and revelation, transcends the ordinary to become a saga of sonic wisdom and regality from an ancient era.

In my alignment with the role God intended for me, I find myself navigating the corridors of time. Inspired by a divine revelation and guided by ancient secrets, I evolve into a custodian of an ancient legacy—a guardian of sonic sovereignty. My metamorphosis echoes the transformation of Sari into Sarah, an evolution intertwined with the melodies of the auditory realm.

Through this journey, I become not just Tashlultum but a vessel for the echoes of the past to resonate in the present and guide the future. My life, intricately woven into the grand symphony, becomes a unique composition—a melodic thread contributing to the eternal tapestry of sound and wisdom that Tashlultum, the Queen of Sound, continues to weave across the cosmic expanse. This preface is a humble attempt to leave behind enough information in my lifetime to explain the unexplainable, ensuring that the resonant legacy of Tashlultum endures.

Acknowledgement

I

I Am Tashlultum

1

In the Shadow of Angels and Serpents

Once upon a time in the vibrant tapestry of my childhood, amidst the backdrop of a small green house in a predominantly black neighborhood, I embarked on a journey that would shape the very essence of my being. This is the story of how Tasha metamorphosed into Tashlultum—a tale that unfolds in the corridors of memory, echoing with the whispers of an angel and the hisses of a snake.

Nestled within the confines of my mother's childhood room in my grandmother's house, a doorknob became the gateway to my own personal Eden. It was a room that witnessed the dance between an ethereal angel and a cunning snake, the dichotomy of light and shadow that would shape the contours of my soul.

The walls of that room held the echoes of profound conversations with my Fairy Godmother—an elusive figure who gifted me a dog, bestowed me with advice beyond my years, and whose presence transcended the boundaries of ordinary companionship. It was she who spoke to me in the language of wisdom, so much so that even my mother recognized the depth of the discourse, seeing beyond the innocent eyes of a child.

But fate, in its mysterious design, dictated that this celestial bond would be ephemeral. The moment arrived when my Fairy Godmother revealed that, although she would forever remain by my side, the curtain of visibility would fall. The realization struck me like a tempest, and tears streamed down my cheeks at the prospect of losing my confidante, my celestial friend.

In the canvas of my grandmother's house, painted white halfway up the trees by my grandfather, this room held the gateway to realms unseen. A tiny living room with a piano to the right, a sofa to the left, and a hallway leading to a world where reality intertwined with the mystical.

The house stood as a solitary emerald in a sea of black, adjacent to a trailer park that separated two worlds—black and white. A physical barrier, a gate, bore witness to the divisive thoughts that lingered in the air, revealing the complex mindset of the neighborhood.

Amidst this dichotomy, the room in which I dwelled told the story of my formative years. A room shared by my mother and aunt in their childhood, it had become my sanctuary—a place where an angel's whispers and a serpent's deceit filled the air. The doorway to my personal Eden, where innocence met wisdom.

As the days unfolded, the boundaries of reality blurred. A peculiar incident marked my perception—a vision of my grandfather, seemingly tangible, yet devoid of substance. Even as a child, I sensed the disquieting truth—that this spectral figure, resembling my granddaddy, was not quite right.

The room, once a haven of celestial discourse, now bore witness to the mysteries of a world beyond the mundane. And so, my childhood unfolded in the company of an angel, a snake, and the unspoken enigma of a ghostly presence that hinted at a destiny yet to unfold.

This is the genesis of Tashlultum—an odyssey that began in the sanctity of childhood, where the mundane and the mystical coalesced, setting the stage for the transformative chapters yet to come. And as I reflect upon those early years, I find answers in the innocence of a child's acceptance, understanding why Eve, too, was unstartled by the serpent's words—because, in the realm of childhood, acceptance is woven into the very fabric of reality.

2

Tashlultum's Nightmare Unfolds

As the whispers of my childhood faded into the tapestry of memory, the next chapter of my life unfolded in the harsh reality of a nightmare. At the tender age of 12, I found myself at the wrong place at the wrong time, a victim of a heinous act that would forever alter the course of my journey.

The trauma of that dark incident cast a long shadow, lingering like a haunting melody in the background of my existence. To compound the pain, life took an unexpected turn, and soon after, I found myself grappling with the responsibilities of motherhood. Two children born out of wedlock marked a challenging chapter in my story, a period of spiraling turmoil and the harsh realization that life's path was not always paved with gentleness.

In the aftermath of the assault, my life took a tumultuous turn. The sanctuary of my grandmother's house became a distant memory as I navigated through a labyrinth of circumstances. Seeking solace, I turned to my father, a figure absent for much of my upbringing. Little did I know, his world was one of shadows, defined by a clandestine trade that would shape my understanding of the complexities of life.

The revelation of my father's involvement in drug dealing unfolded against the backdrop of my teenage years. In the delicate dance of familial dynamics, I played the role of the oblivious child, concealing the truth I had uncovered. The nightmare deepened as I found myself entangled in a world where innocence was a fleeting luxury.

This period, though rife with challenges, laid the foundation for resilience and self-reliance. Stripped of the coddling that sheltered my siblings, I emerged with a sense of independence that would prove invaluable in the chapters to come.

With the weight of my experiences pressing down, I sought refuge in Job Corps, a haven in Baltimore that offered a chance at independence. It was there that the trajectory of my life shifted once again. Love blossomed in unexpected quarters as I connected with someone from Ethiopia, ushering me into the rich tapestry of Ethiopian culture.

Immersed in a world so different from the one I had known, I found solace and guidance in my partner's sister, who played a pivotal role in my growth. She became the guiding force through the maze of cultural nuances, ultimately shaping the woman I was to become.

The ethereal beauty of the Ethiopian culture became a balm for the wounds of my past. It was a time when I distanced myself from the familiar American landscape and embraced an alternate reality, where the ideals of faith and community bore the imprint of Solomon's legacy.

But life is a journey of twists and turns, and the pull of home beckoned me back to Virginia for a brief interlude. The clash of cultures, the dichotomy of my upbringing, and the clash of identities unfolded against the backdrop of Baltimore, marking a period of self-discovery amidst the chaos.

As the nightmare chapter reached its climax, I found myself standing at the crossroads of identity, shaped by Judaism, the Ethiopian faith, and the scant exposure to mainstream Christianity. The three stages of life—innocence, nightmare, and the unknown—charted the course of my existence, each leaving an indelible mark on the woman who would come to be known as Tashlultum.

3

Visions Beyond Time: Tashlultum's Spiritual Odyssey

In the aftermath of the tumultuous period of my nightmare, a brief return home marked a pivotal chapter in my journey. By then, I had begun to grasp the complexities of adulthood, and life presented me with events that would once again alter the trajectory of my existence.

The backdrop of my return home was painted with the hues of spiritual transformation. My father, once immersed in the shadows of a clandestine world, had undergone a profound metamorphosis. His newfound relationship with God had become the focal point of his existence, and the spiritual fervor that now enveloped him spilled into every corner of our lives.

Prayer became the cornerstone of our shared existence. Hours upon hours were dedicated to fervent communion with the divine. In the ethereal ambiance of a beachside hotel that doubled as a temporary haven, I found myself immersed in a realm where visions unfolded like delicate petals.

Virginia Beach became the canvas where my visions painted their most vivid strokes. The proximity to the water seemed to amplify the whispers of the spiritual realm, blurring the lines between reality and the ethereal. Fasting became a conduit for heightened visions, where the boundaries of what was tangible and what existed in the realm of dreams began to blur.

Amidst this tapestry of visions, I encountered prophecies that unfolded in layers of meaning. One poignant dream unveiled the future arrival of another child, a little girl whose presence would grace my life years later. Another vision, however, carried a heavier weight—a child born in the back of a church, whose eyes bore the gray hue of an ethereal departure. A son who transcended the physical realm before drawing his first breath.

The pinnacle of these visions unfolded in a celestial room, where angels stood sentinel on either side. A podium adorned with a large book beckoned, its pages filled with symbols beyond my comprehension. As the voice of God or an angel urged me to read, their breath breathed life into the cryptic symbols, revealing a narrative that unfolded in three sacred chapters.

This celestial encounter marked a turning point, a revelation that transcended the confines of time. The angels, colossal in their divine presence, knelt as I walked a path between them, towards the sacred book. The echoes of that celestial room resonated in my being, becoming a compass that guided me through the labyrinth of life.

Returning to Baltimore with these visions imprinted on my soul, my life took an unexpected turn once more. Living with my boyfriend and his family, the dreams and visions continued, but with a disconcerting twist. Time seemed to warp and overlap as if caught in the throes of a cosmic dance. I would dream, awaken, and find myself reliving moments with a peculiar déjà vu.

It was a surreal experience where the fabric of time seemed malleable, bending and folding upon itself. Conversations echoed, actions replayed, and I found myself navigating a landscape where the boundary between past and present blurred. The cosmic rewind, a recurring phenomenon, bestowed upon me glimpses of the unfolding future, leaving me in a state of bewilderment.

In this mystical tapestry, conversations with God, dreams, and visions became intertwined with the mundane, forging a reality where the ethereal and the everyday coexisted seamlessly. Little did I know that this extraordinary connection with the divine would set the stage for the chapters yet to be written.

4

Echoes of Loss: The Ordeal of Timothy's Passing

The year was 2006, and the landscape of my life had shifted once more, painted with hues of love, marriage, and the anticipation of a new life. Remarried, I found myself nestled in the embrace of matrimony, with a daughter who we call Ali (Erica Alejandra), a manifestation of a vision, and a son, Timothy Isaiah, awaiting his grand entrance into the world.

Life had stationed us in Louisiana, a state still recovering from the ravages of a recent flooding. As the murky waters receded, leaving behind a haunting graveyard of dead trees, my journey took an unforeseen turn. Louisiana (Hurricane **Katrina August and September 2005)**, with its scars still healing, became the backdrop for an event that would shatter the tranquility of our military existence.

My ninth month of pregnancy unfolded with a persistent unease. Something felt amiss, a maternal intuition that refused to be silenced. The military pace, the unfamiliarity of part-time medical practitioners, and the lingering aftermath of the floods set the stage for a harrowing ordeal.

Frequent visits to the doctor painted a picture of dismissiveness. The medical professional, ensconced in an "it'll be alright" attitude, failed to grasp the urgency that echoed in my maternal instincts. The situation took a darker turn when the doctor's demeanor shifted, transforming her words into a cruel refrain, questioning my comprehension of the gravity of the situation.

It was amidst this atmosphere of uncertainty that a vision visited me. In a luminous realm of white hallways, a distant relative, a male cousin, delivered a haunting message—Timothy's heartbeat was dwindling. The weight of impending tragedy hung in the air as he urged me to brace for what lay ahead.

Awakening from this ethereal encounter, I rushed to the living room, emotions unraveling. In desperate pleas, I beseeched God to spare my son's life. Silence reigned until, with a thunderous voice, God posed a question laden with consequences, a question that pierced the veil of my understanding.

"Are you willing to take the consequences if I do as you ask?"

In the absence of precedent, fear and confusion gripped me. The unknown consequences loomed, and with a vulnerable trust, I yielded to a divine will beyond my comprehension. I rested for what was to come next.

Upon waking up, my husband rushed me to the ER during this hospital visit, propelled by premonitions and guided by a mother's intuition. However, my apprehensions faced skepticism upon arrival. The disheartening revelation of Timothy's diminishing life reverberated through the sterile corridors, delivered with a chilling detachment. Amidst this somber setting, a new doctor, responsive to my distress, emerged on the scene. In stark contrast to the prior indifference, this compassionate healer displayed unwavering empathy, offering resolute support through the impending ordeal.

The heart-wrenching process of delivering Timothy unfolded, a journey through grief and acceptance. During pain and loss, I discovered a strength within, a resilience that transcended the boundaries of human endurance.

This pivotal period, etched in the chapters of my life, tested the limits of heart-break and survival. Timothy's passing left an indelible mark, echoing beyond the confines of grief and into the realm of understanding the unfathomable consequences of choices made in the crucible of despair.

5

Navigating Life's Unseen Currents

In 2010, a profound chapter unfolded in my life, shaping my destiny once again. Filled with a yearning to expand my family, I embarked on the journey of adoption. My heart sought a child, one akin to Ali's age, hovering around six to seven years old. As I traversed an overpass one day, my gaze turned skyward, and to my astonishment, beheld two colossal rainbows stretching across the expanse, a sight so magnificent it demanded a pause. Intrigued by the Biblical symbolism of rainbows as a covenant, I pondered its significance for my own life.

> ***genesis 9:12–17*** *CEV The rainbow that I have put in the sky will be my sign to you and to every living creature on earth. It will remind you that I will keep this promise forever. When I send clouds over the earth, and a rainbow appears in the sky, I will remember my **promise** to you and to all other living creatures*

The divine message seemed clear—a promise that the sorrows akin to the loss of my beloved Timothy would not recur. The notion of receiving double blessings after adversity lingered in my mind. Soon after, a call came, altering the course of my life. "We have two newborns, just three days old. Are you interested?" Without hesitation, my resounding "yes" echoed, sealing my commitment to these two precious souls.

Anna and Man, the monikers I bestowed upon them, would become the source of profound healing. Unbeknownst to me at the time, these names echoed an ancient lineage—Enduanna, a daughter, and Manish, a son, from a distant past life as Tashlultum. The dual blessing not only filled the void left by Timothy but also opened my heart to love anew.

Timothy's memory persisted, etched in the depths of my soul, and grieving became an arduous journey. In an attempt to aid another grieving soul, I created a graphic book for a grieving mother, infusing lightness into the memories of her departed child. Yet, the wounds in my heart lingered.

A pivotal moment ensued when, in a fit of despair, I audibly declared to God that He didn't love me. The palpable pain in the room, as if I had wounded the divine, struck me to the core. Swiftly, I recanted, acknowledging my inability to comprehend His actions. In response, a directive echoed—pick up the Bible and read. Skeptical but compelled, I did so, making the sacred text a nightly ritual. Writing down interpretations through the lens of my experiences, I found solace and understanding. The adoption of the twins became not just an expansion of my family but a profound path to healing, merging the divine promise of rainbows with the enduring power of love.

6

The Symphony of Sozo Keys

In the intricate weave of my life, the year 2012 marked a turning point, linking the threads of the past to future events. Commencing like any ordinary year, it unfolded as the canvas for an extraordinary creation.

Motivated by the desire to convey the depths of the Bible to my children, I embarked on a mission to craft a game that would breathe life into its stories. As a fervent reader of the Bible, intricate patterns within its verses began to catch my eye. During one of these moments of revelation, a gentle nudge prompted me to explore beyond the pages and go to my piano.

What transpired next was the birth of a captivating concept: a game based on the seven days of creation, a recurring theme in both the Bible and the calendar. Seven days, echoing the seven notes on a piano, resonating within an octave of twelve keys, mirroring the months in a year. The divine connection became apparent, a musical revelation.

With enthusiasm bubbling, I delved into the creation of a piano game, a synthesis of biblical tales, numerology, and animal symbols drawn from the Torah. Each note transformed into a character, from the first note symbolizing Abraham, akin to a dog or a wolf, to subsequent characters aligning with biblical figures in their chronological order.

This game, named Sozo Keys, became a bridge between the biblical narratives and the art of playing the piano. By converting sheet music into a color-coded language inspired by the coat of many colors, my children could now play instantly. The prism of colors on their piano keys represented the prism of the coat, unveiling Christ in the white light at the game's culmination.

The Sozo Keys system, my brainchild, blended music, numerology, and biblical symbolism, transcending a mere piano practice tool. It became a captivating educational game, transforming the way my children engaged with the Bible and the piano.

As my kids embraced the piano with newfound enthusiasm, I contemplated expanding their learning experience. The notion of incorporating aural learning surfaced, prompting me to encourage them to listen to the piano before playing—a layer I hadn't explored fully at that point.

Simultaneously, a scientific exploration unfolded, drawing parallels between the patterns in the Torah and the patterns in scientific disciplines. Sozo Keys, initially rooted in the joy of playing piano, evolved into a multidimensional learning experience, blending spirituality, art, and science.

Reflecting on this journey, I realized the profound connection between heaven and earth, mirrored yet distinct. The piano, akin to the earth, and the sheet music, representative of the heavens, coexisted in harmony. To facilitate this understanding, I innovatively color-coded the sheet music to match the piano keys, simplifying the learning process.

The Sozo Keys invention not only facilitated piano proficiency but became a portal to a deeper comprehension of the sacred texts. As the colors danced between the sheet music and the piano, a symphony of understanding resonated in the hearts of my children.

This exploration began in 2012, marking a testament to a journey of discovery, creativity, and a harmonious blend of spirituality and art. The Sozo Keys game continues to echo through our home, an ever-evolving melody that connects my children to the rich threads of biblical tales, each note a stepping stone on their musical and spiritual journey.

7

The Night the Cosmos Spoke

In the realm of my life's chronicles, the year 2012 etched a significant chapter, connecting the dots between past and future events, threading through the fabric of nine years until the pivotal juncture of 2021. This narrative unfolds in the landscape of Chesterfield, Virginia, where a seemingly ordinary night transcended into an extraordinary celestial symphony.

While nestled in the comfort of my bed, the stillness of the night was shattered by a resounding noise that echoed across the realms. Its intensity was so profound that it seemed to reverberate globally, an audible cosmic wave disrupting the tranquility of sleep. Astonishingly, my husband lay undisturbed, oblivious to the cosmic overture that enveloped our surroundings.

In stark contrast, my youngest son, Isaiah, one year junior to the twins, was not spared from the cosmic impact. Startled by the celestial resonance, he tumbled from his bed, physically succumbing to the force of the unseen vibrations.

Rushing to his side, I found him in a state of distress. Comforting him, I wondered about the nature of this cosmic phenomenon. A multitude of thoughts swirled in my mind, torn between Christian and Jewish interpretations. Was this the herald of Christ descending from the sky, as Christians believe, or an enlightenment foretold in Jewish teachings? In the midst of this internal conflict, I found myself gazing out of the window, half-expecting a divine light or a celestial being.

Driven by an inexplicable compulsion, I rose from my bed, guided by the instinct to pray. In the quiet of the night, seeking answers, I posed my questions to the divine. In a hushed, gentle voice—a whisper more felt than heard—I received an explanation. Assignments had been distributed, reserved for those in their rightful places. An assignment for every soul, a cosmic task to fulfill.

In this divine allocation, my son Isaiah, still in the early bloom of youth, was unable to comprehend and receive his assignment. His cry, a testament to the weight of the cosmic message that eluded him at his tender age.

Within the walls of our home, only two souls resonated with the cosmic assignment—Isaiah and myself. Despite his youth, Isaiah exhibited signs of a unique calling, hidden even within the realms of video games. Scriptures concealed within pixels hinted at a spiritual journey yet to fully unfold.

As days unfolded into a gentle rhythm, a gradual revelation unfolded. A newfound connection with the divine was established every Sabbath, a day woven into the fabric of our lives. The Lord's directive echoed through the sacred stillness of the Sabbath, urging me to uphold its sanctity.

Noticing a pattern, the floodgates of inspiration opened each Friday, setting the stage for the Sabbath to come. The day, with its inherent significance for Levites, unfolded as a canvas for spiritual revelations. An unusual nervous anticipation, unveiled by my husband, signaled the impending flow of divine insights.

Sabbath transformed from a tradition into a reservoir of spiritual revelations. It became a day of family, study, and a sacred influx of divine wisdom. The Levite connection, evident in the synchronicity of the day, laid the foundation for a spiritual journey enriched by the rhythms of faith.

This, however, was merely the prelude to the subsequent chapter of my spiritual voyage, an expedition into realms yet to be unveiled.

8

Whispers of the Cosmos: Unveiling the Sound of Creation

In the tapestry of my life, the year 2021 stands as a profound chapter, a year cloaked in the shadow of a global pandemic. COVID-19 had confined the world to the walls of isolation, and within those confines, a journey of unparalleled insight unfolded.

As the world grappled with uncertainty, my family and I found ourselves navigating the uncharted territories of lockdown. The outside world faded into a distant memory, while within the walls of our home, a cascade of profound events was set into motion.

My study sessions, initiated during this period, became a gateway to a realm beyond the ordinary. It felt as though I had become a vessel for information, a conduit between the cosmic symphony and the tangible world. Day and night, revelations poured into my consciousness, compelling me to rise from my slumber, the ink of inspiration flowing onto the pages beside my bed.

The crux of this newfound knowledge was rooted in the language of sound. Through my creation, the Sozo Keys, a musical language resonating with synesthetic brilliance, I embarked on a journey to decipher the cuneiform language of the universe. Each key held a profound meaning, transcending the boundaries of mere musical notes. As I unraveled the mysteries encoded within, the characters and stories formed around each key, bringing forth an understanding that surpassed the superficial.

In the labyrinth of ancient symbolism, I discovered a language that spoke of different realms and stages of evolution. The Torah, my guide in this odyssey, unveiled the symbolism of the cat—an emblem of the mind's rebirth, its nine lives echoing the cyclical nature of mental evolution.

The calendar, a celestial tapestry, presented a rhythmic dance of planets and stars, each note in harmony with the universe. The natural energies coursing through certain days offered a key to unlocking optimal thinking, actions, and connections with others.

Yet, amidst this symphony of cosmic revelations, a pivotal moment shattered the veil of skepticism regarding past lives. A vivid night, choked by the sensation of a telescope thrust into my throat, marked the awakening of a connection to a previous existence. The akashic records,(They are believed by theosophists to be encoded **in a non-physical plane of existence known as the mental plane**. Because it is believed that the records are encoded vibrationally into the inherent fabric of space, some have likened the mechanism as similar to how holograms are created) a revelation in the dream, hinted at the intricacies of a past life, a life once lived as Tashlultum.

This journey is a testament to the pains endured, a journey that transcends the earthly realm into the celestial. The information I carry is a fusion of agony and enlightenment, a mosaic of revelations born from the crucible of hardship.

As I document this narrative, I am acutely aware that the past is a guide, a roadmap to my evolution into Tashlultum. This is not a proclamation of perfection but an acknowledgment of imperfections and the transformative power of wisdom born from adversity.

This is the commencement of my odyssey into Tashlultum, an evolution fueled by the rhythm of the cosmos, the resonance of sound, and the unwavering connection to the divine.

9

Echoes of Loss: Navigating Grief in 2022

The year 2022 emerged as a pivotal chapter, etched with profound events that would alter the trajectory of my journey. It all began with a dream—a vision of a colossal angel wielding a sword, severing homes. Little did I know, this dream foreshadowed a year cloaked in the shadows of mortality.

The year unfolded with a series of losses, each more poignant than the last. Childhood friends, family members, and mentors departed, leaving a void that echoed with the solemnity of farewell. Among them, my uncle, a figure almost akin to a brother, succumbed to cancer in a swift and merciless manner, leaving me grappling with the abruptness of life's fragility.

Amidst these heart-wrenching departures, a fateful day unfolded when I agreed to accompany my aunt to a funeral. Little did I know that this would be a day etched in grief. While at the service, my aunt, who had retired and was striving to reclaim her health, suddenly fell ill. The bathroom became a silent witness to her struggle, a struggle that transcended the boundaries of life and death. Despite my efforts, I stood helpless as life slipped away.

The weight of the losses was staggering—each departure marked not only by sorrow but also by lessons and revelations. My aunt, a force in my life, had imparted wisdom in the most challenging of times. Even in the face of disagreements, her insistence on love and familial bonds remained unwavering, challenging me to embrace forgiveness and understanding.

As grief gripped my heart, I turned to the teachings of Judaism, a guide that offered both solace and a roadmap for the grieving soul. With a resolve rooted in tradition, I granted myself a year to mourn, a year to grapple with the intricacies of loss. This structured approach, a gift from Jewish customs, proved instrumental in navigating the labyrinth of sorrow.

In the depths of despair, a beacon of support emerged in the form of an unexpected ally—a coach whose words transcended religious differences. Her guidance, even through Christian literature, provided a fresh lens through which to view my pain. Amidst the pages, I found perspectives that resonated, offering a lifeline when I needed it the most.

As the healing journey unfolded, a revelation surfaced—one that challenged my perspective on control and acceptance. The struggle with my uncle's choice of treatment became a metaphor for relinquishing control, a lesson in embracing the organic path each individual chooses. The realization that some narratives cannot be controlled, no matter how desperately we wish to dictate them, brought a transformative shift in my outlook.

The tapestry of grief, woven with threads of pain and profound insights, was both an ode to the departed and a testament to the resilience of the human spirit. In the crucible of loss, I found not only sorrow but also the seeds of growth, sown by the wisdom of those who walked alongside me.

"Echoes of Loss: Navigating Grief in 2022" stands as a testament to the universal journey of grief, the shared human experience that binds us in our vulnerabilities and strengthens us in our ability to heal.

10

Insights into Life's Mysteries

Now that we've delved into the tapestry of my background, blemishes and all, it's time to unravel the symphony that is Tashlultum—a name bestowed upon me by the divine. God, in His mysterious ways, revealed that this was not just a name but a connection to a past life, a notion I once found hard to embrace. Yet, when divine revelations are handed to you, skepticism takes a back seat, and acceptance becomes the only path.

My narrative unfolds in a series of short stories—much like chapters in the Bible. These stories aren't just about me; they're about my people, the black community. Presented to me as if they were children's tales, they carry undertones of religious essence and layers of historical significance. To decipher their true depth, one must grasp the identities behind the archetypes within these mythical narratives.

Picture it like learning music—54 keys, 54 stories, and 54 sounds, each demanding explanation. This is where we begin, at the genesis, just as the Lord unfolded it for me. In the world of sound, my children learn through the piano. Playing scales, understanding octaves, and numbering the keys from 1 to 7—the beginning stages of recognizing the seven notes on the piano. But hold on, our piano note doesn't start with A; it starts with C. So, C, D, E, F, G, A, B—assigned numbers for clarity. These numbers repeat, creating the foundation for the stories we are about to explore.

Now, we focus solely on the white keys, the basics. We align the seven notes with numbers, give them colors, identify their octaves, and offer a concise summary. Each note embodies an archetype, akin to unraveling an alphabet with each letter telling a unique, complete story. For instance, C, equivalent to Abraham, symbolizes the tribe of Judah—feminine energy personified in the cat.

As we progress through the keys, D, represented by the dog, echoes the seed of the tribe—Isaac. E, the elephant, embodies Jacob, with its split personality akin to the bull. F, the fish, represents Moses, the one navigating life's circular currents. G, the giraffe, signifies David. The ape, the most intelligent creature, is Solomon. And finally, B, the bear, symbolizes Christ, embodying the preparation for lean times and the promise of rest.

The structure of these stories unfolds with intention. Abraham, Isaac, Jacob, Moses, David, Solomon, and Christ—seven keys, seven archetypes, each contributing to a grander melody. The giraffe, representing David, guides us in understanding the intelligence and resilience required to navigate life's challenges. Solomon, the apex of intellect embodied in an ape, reveals that wisdom is the key to unlocking life's mysteries.

In the grand scheme, the bear, a symbol of Christ, carries honey within—a metaphorical sustenance to prepare for the winters of life. It encapsulates the concept of planning during good times to navigate the bad. Just as the seven good years precede the seven years of famine, the seven keys echo the rhythm of preparation and the importance of knowledge in facing impending challenges.

In understanding the foundation of these seven keys—C, D, E, F, G, A, B—we find a harmonious convergence of music, numerology, and archetypes. These keys, when explored with depth, offer a lens into the intricacies of existence, providing not just notes but a resonance with the human experience. This, my friend, is the beginning—a prelude to the stories that follow, each with its own unique melody, unraveling the mythos of life and sound.

11

The Harmonic Odyssey of Abraham:

As the chords of Tashlultum's symphony resonate, we find ourselves immersed in the intricacies of her narrative—a tale woven with threads of divine revelation and historical depth. Like a musical journey, we've traversed the white keys, each note a portal to a profound archetype. But the melody doesn't end here; it evolves, embracing the shadows and the brilliance that lie ahead.

Our exploration begins with C, the embodiment of Abraham and the tribe of Judah—a fusion of feminine energy personified in the regality of a cat. This key not only carries the weight of ancestral identity but serves as a testament to the resilience of a community marked by its unique vibrancy.

Moving to D, represented by the loyal dog, we encounter the seed of the tribe—Isaac. This note echoes through time, a reminder of the importance of loyalty and the continuity of a legacy. The canine loyalty mirrors the steadfast commitment to preserving heritage and passing it down through generations.

E, the majestic elephant and the archetype of Jacob, leads us into the realm of duality. Just as the elephant boasts strength and wisdom, Jacob embodies a dual nature—a theme intricately woven into the fabric of existence. The bull's persona merges seamlessly with the contemplative, creating a harmonious dichotomy.

The fish, our fourth note, mirrors the circular journey of Moses navigating life's currents. As Moses circled in the dance of destiny, so does the fish in its aqueous realm. The circular narrative becomes a metaphor for life's cyclical nature, urging us to navigate the currents with resilience and purpose.

G, the towering giraffe symbolizing David, takes center stage. This key encapsulates the intelligence and resilience needed to overcome life's challenges. Like the giraffe, reaching new heights requires an upward gaze, a vision that transcends the ordinary—a quality that defines the spirit of David.

Solomon, the apex of intellect personified in an ape, resides in the note A. This key serves as a reminder that wisdom is the master key unlocking life's mysteries. The resonance of intellect echoes through the ages, inviting us to seek understanding and enlightenment.

B, the bear symbolizing Christ, emerges as the final note, carrying honey within—a metaphorical sustenance for life's winters. The bear's wisdom lies in planning during times of abundance, a lesson mirrored in the seven good years preceding the seven years of famine. Christ's symbolism extends beyond religion, embracing universal principles of foresight and preparation.

As the seven keys harmonize, a tapestry unfolds—a tapestry that binds the tales of Abraham, Isaac, Jacob, Moses, David, Solomon, and Christ. This tapestry, woven with the threads of sound, numerology, and archetypes, resonates with the essence of human experience.

The resonance within these keys is not confined to the melody but extends to the core of our existence. It beckons us to listen not just with our ears but with our hearts and souls. In the chapters that follow, we shall continue this journey, each note revealing a new layer, a new revelation, until the symphony of Tashlultum's narrative reaches its crescendo.

12

The Harmonic Tapestry Unveiled

In the rich tapestry of life, unlocking profound insights requires the ability to discern patterns—the hidden melodies that weave through our existence. Just as the ancient Greek mathematician Protagoras did, we can pause to listen to the rhythmic beats of life and unveil the harmonies that echo within our surroundings.

Protagoras' journey began with a humble blacksmith's shop, where the rhythmic hammering produced a note, an octave higher, as it struck the metal. This seemingly mundane observation propelled Protagoras into a realm of exploration, delving into the intricate correlation between the size of an object and the tones it produced. His experiments involved plucking strings and striking vessels filled with various liquids, unraveling the mathematical relationship between objects and sound.

Inspired by Protagoras' revelations, Pythagoras took the stage. He took two strings of identical material, one twice the length of the other, and as he plucked them, the shorter string vibrated at twice the frequency of the longer one—resulting in the creation of an octave, an interval of eight tones. This exploration of ratios revealed the musical beauty hidden in the relationships between different lengths of strings.

But this journey into harmonics is not just a historical tale; it's a key to understanding the present. In our modern lives, these ancient patterns offer guidance for transformative solutions. Whether unraveling the complexities of our grocery bills or navigating the challenges of daily existence, the harmonic blueprint stands as a timeless guide to unlock the symphony within our lives.

The Arcadian people, masters of sound, held a unique position in this grand symphony. Contrary to common beliefs suggesting they worshiped gods, they revered masters—individuals skilled in comprehending the intricate dance of harmonics. The rise of the Arcadian Empire wasn't just a conquest; it was a harmonious exchange of knowledge with other tribes. Each tribe contributed its unique insights, fostering a land where diverse tribes coexisted, each with a specific role and purpose.

Fast forward to the present day, where understanding these ancient patterns can lead us towards transformative solutions. As we stand at the crossroads of our existence, the harmonies of the past can guide us into creating a harmonious future.

The Artistry of Harmonic Blueprint

The harmonic blueprint, like an intricate melody, unfolds its layers of wisdom. It's more than a historical narrative; it's a living guide to orchestrate the symphony of our daily lives. Let's explore the artistry of this harmonic blueprint, resonating from the past into the present.

Protagoras' Acoustic Odyssey

Imagine the bustling ancient streets where Protagoras walked, his keen ears attuned to the symphony of life. The blacksmith's shop, a modest yet resonant chamber, became the backdrop for Protagoras' acoustic odyssey. The rhythmic clangs of the hammer, seemingly chaotic, held within them a hidden order—a pattern discernible to the astute observer.

As Protagoras experimented with plucking strings and striking vessels filled with an array of liquids, he revealed the mathematical relationships between object sizes and the tones they produced. The ordinary became extraordinary as he uncovered the harmonies encoded in the very fabric of existence.

Pythagorean Serenade

Pythagoras, inspired by Protagoras' revelations, stepped onto the stage of discovery. Armed with two strings of identical material—one twice the length of the other—he embarked on a serenade of mathematical proportions. The resonance of the shorter string, vibrating at double the frequency of the longer one, birthed the octave, an eight-tone interval that echoed through the ages.

The exploration of ratios became Pythagoras' musical canvas. Different lengths of strings produced harmonies, revealing the hidden order in the universe's grand composition. The artistry of Pythagorean serenades lay in the precision of ratios—their delicate dance creating a symphony that transcended mere notes.

The Arcadian Overture

Within the grand tapestry of history, the Arcadian people played a distinct overture. Far from conventional beliefs, they didn't worship gods but esteemed masters—those fluent in the language of harmonics. The rise of the Arcadian Empire wasn't marked solely by conquest; it was a harmonious collaboration, an exchange of knowledge with diverse tribes.

This unique empire, a mosaic of tribes each contributing its melody, showcased the beauty of harmonious coexistence. The symphony they created wasn't just audible in the sound waves but resonated in the very ethos of their shared existence. The Arcadian overture wasn't about dominance but about the interplay of diverse notes, creating a collective masterpiece.

The Harmonic Blueprint Today

In the present day, the echoes of Protagoras' and Pythagoras' discoveries reverberate. The harmonic blueprint, once the guide to an ancient symphony, remains relevant, offering insights into modern challenges. From the complexities of our grocery bills to the intricate dance of life's dilemmas, the harmonic blueprint serves as a compass, pointing us toward transformative solutions.

Consider, for instance, the mundane yet universal challenge of managing grocery bills. In the harmonious dance of numbers, there exists a pattern, a rhythm that, when discerned, allows for transformative solutions. Let's journey through the practical application of the harmonic blueprint in the realm of grocery shopping, where the rhythmic beats of ancient wisdom still find resonance.

Grocery Shopping Symphony

Embarking on the journey of the seven days, we weave a practical symphony of grocery planning. In this modern alchemy, we craft a meticulously detailed menu for the week—a reflection of the mathematical precision found in ancient harmonics. Just as Pythagoras found ratios in string lengths, we find a balance in our grocery list, aligning needs with wants, creating a harmonious composition.

The execution of our plan becomes a ritual—an orchestrated ballet through the aisles of the supermarket. Each item carefully selected is a note in the larger melody of our culinary week. The resonance of our choices extends beyond mere sustenance; it echoes in the financial harmony of our budget.

As we become connectors in this symphony, bridging the gap between our actions and their impact on our families, we embody the spirit of the Arcadian people. It's not just about filling the cart; it's about orchestrating a harmonious link between our daily choices and our greater purpose. The grocery list transforms into a score, and every purchase becomes a deliberate note, contributing to the overall composition of our lives.

Spiritual Commitment in the Aisles

Yet, the grocery store aisles are not just physical spaces; they become arenas of spiritual commitment. Rain or shine, abundance or scarcity, we adhere to our grocery plan with unwavering dedication. The discipline of consistency becomes a form of spiritual practice—an acknowledgment of the rhythms embedded in our lives.

As we progress through the seven days of our culinary symphony, a gift unfolds—the gift of discipline. Just as Moses circled the mountain, our daily journey becomes a ritual of climbing. Each day, we master the art of planning, acting, connecting, finding purpose, and embracing spirituality. The grocery store transforms into a temple, and our choices become offerings in the sacred dance of daily existence.

Preparing for Tomorrow

As the seventh day approaches, we prepare for tomorrow. Like the bear stockpiling for winter, we stock our pantry, ensuring that our moments of abundance extend into potential moments of scarcity. The seven-day alchemy,

way to control the masses or to keep people focused on their individual tasks. Now, imagine applying this ancient wisdom not just to grocery bills but to various aspects of your life.

Let's delve deeper into the practicality of this approach by continuing with our grocery bill example. You've crafted a plan, executed it, connected it to feeding your family, embraced it religiously, and now you're preparing for tomorrow like the bear storing for winter. What if you expand this approach to your finances?

Financial Symphony

Just as you've orchestrated a culinary symphony, imagine applying the same principles to your financial life. Create a monthly plan, detailing your expenses, savings, and investments. Execute this plan diligently, just as you did with your grocery plan. Connect your financial actions to your long-term goals, whether it's buying a home, saving for your child's education, or retiring comfortably.

As you consistently follow your financial plan, you'll begin to accumulate savings—a stockpile for your financial winter. Instead of spending every dime you earn, you set aside a portion for future use, ensuring that your good times extend into potential times of scarcity. The financial bear in you emerges, preparing for unforeseen challenges with the discipline of saving.

Time Alchemy

Now, let's explore the alchemy of time. Your grocery plan has not only saved you money but also time. You're cooking once a week, vacuum sealing, and embracing the freedom that comes with having ready-made meals. Apply this same time alchemy to other areas of your life.

Consider your daily routines. Can you create a weekly plan for your tasks, saving time by batch-processing similar activities? Apply this to work, where the principles of planning, action, connecting, purpose, and spirituality can enhance your productivity and efficiency. The ancient pattern of seven days becomes a guide, ensuring that you allocate your time wisely and consistently.

Harmonizing Relationships

Extend the ancient wisdom to relationships. Craft a plan for quality time with your loved ones, execute it with sincerity, connect emotionally, and embrace the discipline of consistent bonding. Your relationships become a harmonious symphony, with each note contributing to the overall melody of a fulfilling and connected life.

Purposeful Living

The overarching purpose of this ancient wisdom is to guide you toward purposeful living. As you navigate the seven days, you not only cut your grocery bill but unlock a blueprint for intentional, harmonious living. The purpose isn't just financial savings; it's the creation of a life where each action aligns with a greater purpose, where the mundane becomes sacred, and where discipline transforms into a spiritual practice.

In conclusion, the seven-day alchemy is a versatile tool, a key that unlocks doors to transformative solutions in various aspects of your life. Whether you're tackling financial challenges, time management, relationship building, or simply seeking a more purposeful existence, the ancient pattern of seven days offers guidance. Embrace the wisdom of the ancients, and let it echo through the tapestry of your life, creating a harmonious symphony of purpose and fulfillment.

1 (Sunday)
   Leadership and initiation
   2 (Monday)
   Nurturing and emotional support
   3 (Tuesday)
   Communication and idea-sharing
   4 (Wednesday)
   Organization and practicality

5 (Thursday)
Exploration and knowledge-seeking
6 (Friday)
Relationship-building and harmony
7 (Saturday)
Planning and structuring for the future

II

The 7 Days

13

Navigating the Realms of the Mind

As we embark on the resonant journey within Tashlultum's symphony, exploring Abraham's transformative odyssey through the frequencies C1 to C8, we encounter more than mere musical notes. Instead, we discover thresholds, akin to doors swinging open and closing within the vast expanse of the mind. These symbolic portals offer opportunities for mental ascension, guiding us through crucial junctures in the Torah and tracing the profound stages of Abraham's extraordinary journey.

In Genesis 12:1, the New International Version recounts the divine directive to Abram, a command that echoes the essence of mental transcendence: "Go from your country, your people, and your father's household to the land I will show you." This call to leave behind the familiar—ancestral ties, cultural roots, and familial foundations—is the very essence of what it means to become a thinker. Abraham, in surrendering the known, exemplifies the courage to walk away from everything he thought he knew, including the deeply ingrained beliefs of his father and mother.

In the echoing corridors of Tashlultum's symphony, Abraham's story becomes a resonant testament to the transformative power of relinquishing the familiar. It becomes an invitation to open mental doors, allowing the mind to venture into the unknown, to release preconceptions, and to embrace the mysteries that lie beyond the comfort of what is known.

The divine command to Abram encapsulates the journey of a thinker—the willingness to detach from the security of one's country, people, and familial heritage. It marks a departure from the well-trodden paths of conventional wisdom, beckoning the mind to set forth into uncharted territories, trusting in the guidance of an unseen destination.

Abraham's odyssey, much like the frequencies from C1 to C8, symbolizes a mental sojourn where doors swing open, and the mind steps into the realm of uncertainty. It embodies the courage to transcend mental boundaries, to become a thinker by challenging the very foundations of one's understanding. As Abraham heeds the divine call, so too does the aspiring thinker heed the inner call to abandon the known, embrace the unfamiliar, and chart a course toward unexplored realms of thought.

In essence, the journey of a thinker, inspired by Abraham's example, is an expedition into the symphony of the mind—an exploration of resonances that extend beyond the confines of what is inherited and known. It is a harmonious dance between letting go and discovering, echoing the divine command that propelled Abraham into the vast expanse of mental ascension: "Go, and I will show you."

Embarking at C1, resonating like the solemn beat of ancient drums, we stand at the genesis of Abraham's expedition. Here, ancestral wisdom echoes, connecting us to the roots of our existence. Much like the patriarch Abraham, C1 becomes the foundational note, a cornerstone grounding us in the timeless stories of our forebearers. It serves as a door to understanding, a portal to ancestral insights that shape the mental landscape.

Advancing to C2, where the resonating tone whispers strength and resilience, the cat's emblem of feminine energy threads through this frequency. This stage becomes a mental action plan, a positive note, but with the potential pitfall of becoming stuck in a mental space, grappling with the challenge of translating ideas into action.

C3, pulsating at the midpoint of our harmonic journey, mirrors the rhythm of a beating heart. Echoing Isaac's loyalty through the canine loyalty of the dog, this frequency becomes a mental exercise in understanding the thinkers one needs to connect with. It signifies a door swinging open, ushering us into the chamber of devotion and familial ties, shaping our mental network.

The majestic resonance of C4, symbolized by the regal elephant and embodying the duality of Jacob, weaves a mental symphony of strength and contemplation. It urges the mind to embrace the dualities that define existence, offering doors that open and close, guiding Abraham's journey through the intricate dance of mental fortitude.

In the circular dance of life, C5 mirrors Moses' journey—a fluid exploration encapsulated in the flowing waters of the fish. This frequency reflects the war of the mind, where many find themselves stuck in mental health issues. It serves as a reminder of the cyclical nature of life's currents, urging adaptation and resilience in the mental realm.

Giraffe-like in its towering resonance, C6 embodies the intelligence and resilience needed to overcome life's challenges. Here, David's spirit reaches new mental heights, serving as a guide to ascend beyond the ordinary. Mental doors of insight and resilience unfold, urging the mind to elevate its understanding of the challenges faced.

C7, resonating with Solomon's wisdom, invites us into the realm of intellect. Symbolized by the apex of wisdom—the ape—this frequency becomes a mental exploration of understanding the difference between knowledge and wisdom. Doors swing open, beckoning the mind to seek intellectual enlightenment and knowledge, embodying the essence of Solomon's profound wisdom.

Finally, the crescendo arrives with C8, symbolizing Christ and the bear. This frequency, carrying honey within, becomes a mental allegory of sustenance for life's winters. It embodies the wisdom of planning during times of abundance, ensuring mental resilience during times of scarcity. Doors of mental preparation and foresight open, providing a pathway to navigate the seasons of life.

Tracing the frequencies from C1 to C8, we bear witness to a harmonic convergence—a door-laden passage through the grand tapestry of Tashlul-tum's narrative. Each note, each mental door, becomes a guide, leading us through the labyrinth of existence, unraveling the symphony of life—one harmonic resonance, one transformative mental door, at a time.

14

A Savvy Approach to Grocery Savings

In the grand symphony of life, understanding patterns can lead us to remark-able insights. Today, let's apply the seven-day alchemy to a practical challenge we all face—reducing our grocery bills. Following a simple plan, we can cut costs without compromising on quality.

Day 1: The Plan

Action:

Create a weekly meal plan for your family. Choose simple recipes with overlapping ingredients to minimize waste. Write down the needed items and quantities for each recipe.

Day 2: Taking Action

Action:

Head to the grocery store armed with your detailed shopping list. Stick to it religiously, avoiding impulse buys. Consider buying generic brands or items on sale to save more.

Day 3: Make the Right Connection

Action:

Connect your grocery purchases to your family's needs. If an item doesn't align with your meal plan, resist the temptation to buy it. Reinforce the connection between your choices and your goal of saving money.

Day 4: The Gift of Savings

Action:

Celebrate the savings you've accumulated by following your plan. Track how much you've saved compared to your usual grocery spending. Consider allocating the extra funds to other financial goals.

Day 5: Spiritual Commitment

Action:

Commit to your new grocery routine religiously. Regardless of external factors, stick to your plan. This consistency will lead to greater savings over time.

Day 6: Preparing for Tomorrow

Action:

Plan for future grocery trips. Reflect on your successful cost-cutting methods and identify areas for improvement. Can you find more affordable alternatives without sacrificing quality?

Day 7: The Bear's Wisdom

Action:

Prepare for unforeseen circumstances. Build a stock of non-perishable items during times of plenty. This ensures you're well-prepared when unexpected challenges arise.

In your seven-day journey, you've transformed the way you approach grocery shopping. By sticking to a well-thought-out plan, you've not only cut costs but also cultivated a mindful connection between your choices and your family's needs. As you prepare for tomorrow, envision a future where your grocery budget becomes a tool for financial freedom and wise spending.

15

The Artistic Venture

In the rhythmic dance of life, where patterns weave profound insights, let's embark on a seven-day alchemy to introduce the harmonies of art into places of worship. Just as we crafted a plan to transform grocery bills, let's now design a transformative plan to bring art into Churches and Synagogues, empowering kids to create, sell, and fund their artistic endeavors.

Day 1: The Vision Unveiled

Plan:

Define your vision. Envision a space where children can unleash their creativity, crafting art that reflects the beauty of spirituality. Consider what art forms you want to introduce—paintings, sculptures, hats, or even books.

Action:

Begin researching various art forms suitable for kids. Identify local artists willing to collaborate and share their expertise. Start mapping out the physical space within the place of worship where the artistic venture will unfold.

Day 2: The Blueprint Takes Shape

Plan:

Create a detailed blueprint of your artistic venture. Outline the steps from setting up art stations to managing sales. Consider how you'll involve the community, inviting kids to participate and congregation members to support.

Action:

Draft a business plan that includes the logistics of the art venture, potential costs, and revenue streams. Reach out to local businesses for potential partnerships or sponsorships to support the venture.

Day 3: Executing the Plan

Plan:

Execute your plan by setting up the art stations, preparing materials, and announcing the artistic venture to the community. Begin promoting the event and encouraging kids to participate.

Action:

Collaborate with local artists to conduct workshops for kids. Set up an online platform for pre-sales of the art pieces to maximize funds raised. Ensure that all materials and logistics are in place for a smooth execution.

Day 4: Connecting Art to Purpose

Plan:

Connect the art venture to a greater purpose. Clearly communicate how the proceeds from the art sales will fund an ongoing art program for kids within the community.

Action:

Create promotional materials that highlight the impact of art on children's development. Share success stories of how art programs have changed lives. Connect with local media to spread the message.

Day 5: Spiritual Discipline in Action

Plan:

Embrace a spiritual commitment to the art venture. Regardless of challenges, stay dedicated to the vision of empowering kids through art. Reinforce the spiritual aspect by involving religious leaders in endorsing the program.

Action:

Reach out to religious leaders to gain their support and endorsement. Organize a brief ceremony or event within the place of worship to spiritually inaugurate the art venture.

Day 6: The Gift of Artistry

Plan:

Recognize and celebrate the artistic gifts within each child. Create a platform where their creativity shines, boosting their confidence and self-esteem.

Action:

Host an art exhibition within the place of worship, showcasing the pieces created by the children. Invite congregation members, parents, and the community to witness the beauty that emerges from the art venture.

Day 7: Preparing for Tomorrow

Plan:

Plan for the future by ensuring the sustainability of the art program. Explore partnerships with local schools, community centers, or art organizations to expand the reach of the program.

Action:

Initiate conversations with potential partners who can support and sustain the art program beyond the initial venture. Develop a strategy for ongoing workshops, exhibitions, and community involvement.

In the symphony of your seven-day alchemy, you've not only introduced art into places of worship but also created a sustainable model where creativity and spirituality intertwine. The artistic venture serves as a beacon of inspiration, showcasing the transformative power of art in the lives of children and the community at large. As you prepare for tomorrow, envision a future where art becomes a driving force for positive change, creating a harmonious tapestry of creativity, purpose, and community support.

16

Harmonizing with the Sound of Creation

In the ancient symphony of life, the cuneiform texts whispered the language of the universe. A profound code, it intertwined numerology, mathematics, and the ethereal melodies of sound. Think of it as cosmic sheet music, where every word was a note, and every note played a song in tune with the universe.

Picture this: your words, your plans, translated into the intricate language of sheet music, resonating with the cosmic vibrations. It's a harmony that aligns your actions with the celestial rhythms. Just like a skilled musician, the ancient scribes ensured that every plan, every intention, was in perfect accord with the universal energy of the day.

Now, let's venture into the essence of the Soto keys—the foundational archetypes that shape our understanding. These archetypes aren't deities but guiding forces, like schoolmasters aiding our remembrance in the grand orchestra of life. So, let's focus on the seven white keys, the seven days of the week, and uncover their fundamental meanings.

Day 1: The Mental Realm - C Note

In our journey through the seven archetypes, we commence with the C note. Imagine it as the core, the mental realm that influences how we think. Whether it's the middle C or C eight, these notes shape the mental plane, orchestrating the symphony of thoughts—positive or negative—that surround us.

Much like the sun's energy, the sound emitted on the day you were born imprints itself on your very being. This energy becomes an integral part of your DNA, influencing your thought processes and mental landscape. So, as you navigate life, be attuned to the echoes of the C note, recognizing its impact on your cognitive symphony.

The Journey of Evolution

The archetypes, like the C note, evolve over time. Abraham, the beginning of a nation, showcases the metamorphosis within these archetypes. Each character, each story is a continuation, a new note building upon the previous one. It's a lesson in understanding the evolution of sound and the shapes it creates.

As you explore the ancient wisdom, remember the importance of these foundational archetypes. They provide the keys to unlock deeper knowledge, much like learning the basics before delving into complexity. Embrace the simplicity, for within it lies the profound wisdom of the ancients.

The Symphony of Shared Energy

Consider the collective energy during your birth—Tor portions, festivals, prayers—all synchronized in a harmonious crescendo. The collective voice influences you, imprints knowledge on your soul, shaping your path and purpose. The interconnectedness of voices speaking in unison amplifies the impact on every soul born under that shared energy.

Harness the power of shared intention and collective thought. Your words, your writings, are the echoes of the cosmic symphony. Write, speak, and express with the awareness that you are contributing to a shared vibration, influencing not just your life but resonating in the universal harmony.

So, as you step into the mental realm of Day 1, understand that your thoughts are notes in the grand symphony of creation. Let the wisdom of the C note guide you on this journey of self-discovery and mindful living.

17

Echoes of the Ancients

In the cosmic chronicles of the Arcadian empire, the ancient language of cuneiform emerges as the transcendent dialect of the universe. To fathom its depths, envision it as the celestial tongue—the intricate script that wove together the very fabric of existence. This language, a cosmic ballet, embraced numerology, mathematics, and the melodious notes of a celestial sheet music.

Consider this: every uttered word transformed into a cosmic melody, resonating through the vast corridors of time. The grand symphony, pulsating with the heartbeat of the universe, harmonized with every celestial note. Should an action falter, an unsynchronized chord disclosed a discordant truth—an inadvertent misstep in the grand composition.

Enter the guardians, entrusted custodians of the cosmic design, ensuring that mortal plans align with the ebb and flow of universal energy. These archetypes, not deities but mentors, stand sentinel in the tapestry of everyday life—a guide through the labyrinth of ancient wisdom.

The archetypes, the Soto keys to healing, cradle a vast knowledge, akin to a foundational understanding before orchestrating a magnum opus. Let's delve into the seven white keys, the archetypes symbolizing the seven days of the week. Each key, a beacon of sound, a fundamental vibration in the cosmic symphony. Their evolution, akin to musical notes on a scale, carries the narrative forward.

Consider Abraham, a mere mortal evolving into the bedrock of a nation—Israel. The narrative unfolds like a melodic progression, each character a note building upon the last. Names morph, roles transform, yet the resonance persists—a continuation in the cosmic melody.

The essence lies in the shapes of sound, the fundamental forms of these archetypes. Middle C, the inaugural note, symbolizes the mental realm—the plane of thought and perception. The influence of these notes, akin to the sun's caress on our skin, shapes the mental tapestry of how we think.

As you contemplate the day of your birth, ponder the sound emitted by the sun at that precise moment. It's not mystical but a scientific dance of cosmic forces. You're born beneath a unique frequency, a melody echoing through your very essence.

The Torah portions, verses chanted during your birth, are resonant echoes influencing your narrative. Envision the collective voices of a community, reciting the same verses, imprinting an indelible mark on your soul. It's not mere ritual; it's a symphony of shared energy sculpting destinies.

Writing, a daily dialogue with oneself, becomes a conduit for self-discovery. Much like the woman in Paris, scribbling seemingly nonsensical thoughts until clarity blossoms. Your words aren't just for you; they are a conversation with greatness, a dialogue with the world.

In the next chapter, our focus shifts to Sunday—the bedrock of the mental plane. As we peer into the essence of this day, we unravel the threads of thought weaving the fabric of existence. The cuneiform symphony persists, and you, my friend, are a vital note in its resounding composition. Let's delve into the foundation of the mental plane, understanding the nuances that shape our very thoughts and existence.

18

Navigating Life's Symphony

In the intricate symphony of thinking, one must carefully orchestrate the elements that contribute to the harmonious melody of life. The journey of thought, akin to the evolution of musical notes from C one to C eight, requires a nuanced understanding and categorization of its diverse components. Despite the inevitability of human error, the endeavor is to place these elements within the appropriate mental framework.

In the modern context, the act of thinking encompasses a myriad of activities, ranging from brainstorming and problem identification to innovation and decision-making. Drawing parallels with the life of Abraham, one wonders if, in our own thinking processes, we sometimes leap ahead without a clear understanding of when and how each facet of thinking should manifest.

Reflecting on the scattering nature of contemporary thinking, the narrative suggests that establishing clarity in defining what is done when and creating conducive environments for specific types of thinking can foster a more organized mental landscape. This introspection invites consideration of the meticulous brainstorming, planning, decision-making, problem-solving, and risk assessment that form the foundation of strategic thinking.

As the narrative unfolds, it explores the expansive realm of thinking, encapsulating various dimensions such as personal philosophies, values, life purpose, ethical frameworks, and effective communication. It delves into the significance of articulating thoughts coherently, whether verbally or in writing, and the emotional intelligence required to express ideas with empathy and self-awareness.

Creativity emerges as a pivotal element, encompassing artistic expressions, innovation, and the invention of solutions. The narrative underscores the importance of recognizing the emotional intelligence required for spontaneous and eloquent articulation, while also emphasizing the need for systematic thinking.

The exploration extends to considerations of personal growth, reflection, goal adjustments, and resilience. Social contributions and responsibilities are contemplated, highlighting the impact of individual voices in a world saturated with generic expressions. The narrative encourages the development of a unique voice, one that transcends the commonplace and speaks to the authenticity of personal experiences and perspectives.

In contemplating the integration of artificial intelligence (AI) into the thinking process, the narrative envisions a collaborative partnership. Rather than fearing AI as a replacement, it is seen as a potential assistant, capable of aligning with an individual's unique way of thinking. The idea of uploading one's thinking framework to AI to generate more personalized responses is presented as a means to streamline and enhance the thinking process.

The narrative circles back to the significance of the Sabbath in shaping thinking. It serves as a reminder of the spiritual nourishment required to guide and evolve one's thought processes. The importance of organizing one's schedule around foundational thinking on the first day of the week is emphasized, creating a structured approach to various aspects of thinking.

In conclusion, the narrative advocates for deliberate and thoughtful thinking, drawing inspiration from the ancient sounds of jazz, particularly the chromatic variety. Listeners are encouraged to immerse themselves in the healing tones of this music while engaging in self-reflection and intentional thought. "Harmony of Thought: Navigating Life's Symphony" thus becomes a journey through the intricate notes of existence, a melody crafted with care, intention, and the harmonious dance of ideas.

III

SOUND ARCHETYPES

a symbolic representation or embodiment of fundamental qualities and meanings associated with sound. It serves as a metaphorical expression that encapsulates the essence, emotional impact, and transformative nature of sound, often conveying cultural, spiritual, or emotional significance. Sound archetypes explore the multifaceted aspects of auditory experiences and their profound effects on human perception and emotion.

<h1 style="text-align:center">19</h1>

The Sonic Symphony: Unraveling the Sound Archetype, Le Cat

In the harmonious realm of ancient Elysium, where the ethereal vibrations of existence intertwined, there existed a peculiar being known as Le Cat. This enigmatic figure, draped in the hues of red, embarked on a sonic journey that resonated with the very fabric of his existence.

Let's delve into the intricacies of what it means to be a Sound Archetype, a manifestation of sound waves and frequencies that dance in the symphony of the mind. Le Cat, the shapeshifter of sounds, epitomized the union of tonal complexities and harmonic revelations.

In the essence of the first C, specifically C5, we unearth the profound significance of sound as a universal language. Le Cat's sonic prowess was not merely about the audible, for in the ancient times, it was believed that numbers themselves had distinct personalities. Le Cat, being associated with numbers, became a living embodiment of these sonic vibrations.

Much like a shape-shifter mastering the art of transforming from one form to another, Le Cat had not fully harnessed the potential of all sounds. His sonic repertoire was a kaleidoscope of frequencies, a journey through the musical scale where each note represented a different facet of his character.

The fourth week of the lunar calendar, a celestial period of heightened energies, marked the crescendo of Le Cat's sonic revelations. The city of Elysium, attuned to the vibrations of the universe, recognized that during this juncture, the veil between dimensions thinned, allowing the true essence of Le Cat's sonic identity to manifest.

Le Cat, in his sonic exploration, mirrored the thoughtful hospitality of Abraham in Genesis 18. The nuances of his sonic dialogue showcased strategic and contemplative thinking, echoing the very essence of the mind as a sonic landscape.

The divine guidance that guided Le Cat through his sonic sojourns echoed the challenges faced by Hagar and Ishmael in the wilderness. The complexities of relationships and the divine interplay of frequencies formed the backdrop of his sonic narrative.

As the chapter of Le Cat unfolded, resonances of the ultimate test akin to Genesis 22 reverberated through the ancient city. The sonic faith of Le Cat faced trials, much like Abraham's belief versus thought dilemma. Sonic vibrations intertwined with profound thinking became the tapestry of his existence.

In understanding the Sound Archetype, Le Cat's sonic landscape offered a glimpse into the multifaceted nature of sound. It symbolized the intricate dance between frequencies, a balance of the sonic pleasure that music brings and the potential for sonic pain when dissonance disrupts the harmony.

The red light, symbolic of passion and pain, painted Le Cat's sonic portrait. Just as red light therapy offers insight into the importance of light, Le Cat's sonic journey highlighted the passion embedded in every note and the potential for pain when dissonant chords played.

As we unravel the sonic symphony of Le Cat, we navigate through the complexities of the mind, where sound becomes a language, a thinker, and a shapeshifter. Le Cat's tale is a sonic odyssey, a journey through the frequencies that echo the very essence of the Sound Archetype.

"Harmony of Thought: Unraveling the Complexities of the Mind Through the C Notes"

In our exploration of the C notes, let's focus on C5 for its symbolic significance. This note emerges in the fourth week of the lunar calendar, corresponding to the fourth Torah portion, known as La Ca t, or "Look at me now."

Week 4

C5- La Cat

1 VAYERA Genesis 18:1-22:24

In the ancient worldview, numbers were believed to possess distinct person-alities. Considering this, the character of the number one, intertwined with zero, holds a special place. Much like the computer's language of ones and zeros expressing vast information, the mind, too, has the ability to articulate a multitude of variables.

Now, delving into the Torah portion, Genesis 18 unfolds a narrative of hospitality and divine dialogue. Abraham's thoughtful actions toward the divine visitors reveal strategic and contemplative thinking. The subsequent shift to the judgment of Sodom and Gomorrah showcases Abraham's nuanced negotiation with God, emphasizing trust and contemplation.

Genesis 21 introduces Sarah's inner struggle with divine guidance, particularly in her relationship with Hagar and Ishmael. Divine communication plays a pivotal role in guiding Hagar and Ishmael through the challenges they face in the wilderness.

The ultimate test of Abraham's faith unfolds in Genesis 22, where he grapples with the divine command to sacrifice his son, Isaac. Abraham's profound thinking reflects the interplay between belief and thought, a testament to his responsibility in shaping three major religions.

The Torah portion underscores the multifaceted nature of decision-making, negotiation with the divine, and the impact of divine communication. It highlights the intricate dance between human and divine intervention in the complex realm of human thinking.

As we consider these figures as characters representing the collective mindset of a nation, we recognize the inherent complexity. Much like the ancient world revered thinkers for their problem-solving abilities, our modern society could benefit from embracing diverse thought patterns for collective growth.

Enter Le Cat, characterized by the color red, symbolizing passion and pain. This figure, a lover in essence, embodies the intricate balance between great love and the accompanying potential for profound pain. In contemplating the mind's complexities, we find parallels in the multifaceted nature of the red key, shedding light on the passionate and, at times, painful aspects of our thinking.

In conclusion, our journey through the C notes unveils the harmony of thought, emphasizing the importance of embracing complexity, diverse perspectives, and the delicate balance between passion and pain within the realm of human thinking.

21

Nigel Miguel Valentine Revell (Sound Archetype KIDS STORY)

Once upon a time, in the ancient Province of Sugar Land, two Merfish's Allace and DeeFlutter, and Liston a Jazz player from the *Black Elephant Jazz troupe* roamed the mystical land. A peculiar sound reached their ears as they strolled through the enchanting Providence of Sugar Land. Allace and DeeFlutter, both merfish, cherished their time together, undisturbed by their differences. Long walks through the magical Providence of Sugar Land were a common joy for the trio.

The odd noise, though heard, did not deter them. They continued their journey until another peculiar sound emerged from behind. This time, all three spun around to uncover the source. To their surprise, a shadowy figure in the brush revealed itself.

"Who's there?" Allace called out.

Anticipation filled their wide eyes as they awaited a response. After a moment, a voice echoed from the shadows, declaring, "It's me, Le' Cat."

Confusion marked Allace's face as she turned to her friends. Suddenly, a tall, black, slinky cat emerged from behind the Walking Tree. Dressed in nickers, a striped vest, and a multicolored hat, Le' Cat walked up and introduced himself.

"I am Nigel Miguel Valentine Revell, but you can call me Le' Cat. At your service," he proclaimed with an exaggerated bow.

Laughter followed his introduction, and the trio curtsied in return. Le' Cat, with pearly white teeth that glittered in the sunlight, inquired about their morning plans.

"Just on a stroll," replied DeeFlutter.

Le' Cat, proud of representing the Third Space of the treble clef Staff, admitted his unique role. Allace, unfamiliar, questioned him, prompting Le' Cat to showcase his mastery as a shape–shifter by changing his clothes with a snap of his fingers. Laughter and joy erupted.

"Turn into something great, like a dragon," suggested DeeFlutter. "No, no… I know, turn into something strong, like an Ox."

Le' Cat, bowing his head in shame, admitted his limited abilities. Disappointment lingered until Le' Cat changed their attire again, transporting them to the Sozo Racetrack. Stunned, the girls clung to each other as they raced around the track, delighting the crowd from the Land of SOZO.

The laughter and excitement continued until Le' Cat, with a snap of his fingers, brought them back to the Sugar Land Province. Returning to normal attire, Le' Cat bid the girls farewell, disappearing for two weeks.

Concerned, Allace asked, "Do you suppose he's alright?"

"I'm sure he's fine," DeeFlutter replied, her tone filled with doubt. The girls continued their day, trying not to worry.

During their routine through the Province of Sugar Land, they spotted a familiar shadow.

"Is that you, Le' Cat?" Allace asked.

"Of course," he replied, emerging from the shadow. With a mischievous grin, Le' Cat proposed a visit to SOZO World.

"Could we?" Allace asked excitedly. With a snap of his fingers, they found themselves in the magical kingdom. Merfish Loops, Muddlefly Fish Water-Slide, Umbrella Jumps, and Elephant Bumper Cars awaited their enjoyment. Their fun was unbelievable.

When ready to leave, Le' Cat snapped his fingers, bringing them back home. Allace expressed her excitement, and Le' Cat, flashing a smile, bid his goodbyes.

Several weeks passed before Le' Cat reappeared, inviting them on a trip under the ocean. Dressed as the Gate Keeper, he played the "Sea" Scale on a beautiful glass piano. Glass doors opened to a passage with mesmerizing creatures like Ear Fish, Rattle Sharks, and Bubble Turtles. They were captivated by the beauty beneath the sea.

As the night concluded, Le' Cat, with a snap of his fingers, brought them home. DeeFlutter, noticing Le' Cat's sadness, touched his hands, experiencing his emotions. Ashamed of his loneliness, Le' Cat explained his heritage and the birthmark in the shape of a heart.

"There is nothing to be ashamed of," DeeFlutter reassured him. "True friendship means that we love you. Come around more, just to hang out. What makes you special is not your ability to change shapes. Can we depend on you?"

"Yes!" Le' Cat exclaimed. DeeFlutter offered her hand, and Le' Cat shook it with a big smile. As they bid their goodbyes, Le' Cat promised to see them tomorrow, chanting, "My name is Nigel Miguel Valentine Revell...but you can call me Le' Cat."

The core theme of the previous Le' Cat story is the exploration and celebration of friendship, acceptance, and the value of individuals beyond their outward abilities or appearances. The narrative revolves around the whimsical adventures of Allace and DeeFlutter with Le' Cat in the mystical Province of Sugar Land. Le' Cat, a shape-shifter with limited abilities, seeks connection and companionship. The story emphasizes:

1. Friendship and Acceptance: Despite their differences, Allace and DeeFlutter cherish their time with Le' Cat. The narrative emphasizes the importance of accepting others for who they are and finding joy in shared experiences.

2. Magical Journeys and Joy: Le' Cat's ability to transform their surroundings and create enchanting adventures showcases the power of imagination and the joy that can be found in simple yet magical moments.

3. Overcoming Loneliness: Le' Cat, initially hiding his loneliness behind magical adventures, opens up to Allace and DeeFlutter. The story highlights the significance of expressing one's emotions, finding understanding friends, and overcoming feelings of isolation.

4. Testing and Strengthening Bonds: The characters go through various adventures, from racing in the Sozo Racetrack to exploring the depths of the ocean. These experiences serve as tests that strengthen the bonds of friendship, trust, and companionship.

5. Self-Acceptance: Le' Cat's unique abilities, symbolized by his shape-shifting, represent the idea that one's uniqueness is something to be celebrated. The story encourages self-acceptance and embracing individuality.

In summary, the core theme of the Le' Cat story is the transformative power of friendship, acceptance, and the joy that comes from connecting with others in a whimsical and magical world. It sends a positive and uplifting message about the value of true companionship and understanding.

22

La Cat Frequency of Love, Fun & Loneliness 523.25 (C5)

Healing Through Sound-523 is a number that follows me a lot because it is my birth number.

The Major things this sound can TRIGGER are "Love and loneliness"

"Much like Le' Cat, the magical guide in our enchanting tale, understanding the causes and effects of the balance between love and loneliness is crucial for individuals seeking to nurture their mental well-being. By recognizing and addressing these factors, much like how Le' Cat navigates the mystical land, individuals can actively work toward achieving a healthier and more balanced mental state. Le' Cat's shape-shifting abilities symbolize the adaptability needed to foster resilience, while his whimsical adventures with Allace and Dee Flutter reflect the importance of building meaningful connections. This guide, inspired by the magical journeys of Le' Cat, aims to provide practical strategies for navigating the challenges of love and loneliness, ultimately promoting overall mental health and fulfillment."

Metaphor List:

1. The Realm of the Mind - Sugar Land: The Tree of lives
   - The mystical Province of Sugar Land serves as a metaphor for the mind—a

realm where thoughts, emotions, and experiences entwine in a captivating symphony.

- Peculiar sounds echo the unexplored facets of the mind, awaiting discovery in the uncharted territories of thoughts and emotions.

2. The Gift Realm of 4F – Merfish:

- The merfish from the Gift Realm of 4F embodies unique talents and perspectives within the mind, enriching the tapestry of thoughts.

- 4F symbolizes a mental state where special gifts and insights reside, contributing to the enchantment of the inner world.

3. Soul Realm: Black Elephant Jazz Players and Chromatic Music:

- The Black Elephant Jazz players harmonize like the chromatic scales, symbolizing the cooperation of various elements in the mind.

- Chromatic music's use of all twelve pitches represents the complexity and richness of thoughts and emotions within the mind, unlocking hidden depths. The black elephants, positioned at 4E on the piano, resonate as key components of this symphony.

4. Le' Cat as a Shape-Shifter – Human Mind:

- Le' Cat's shape-shifting mirrors the ever-changing nature of thoughts and emotions within the mind.

- As a representative of the Third Space of the treble clef Staff, Le' Cat embodies a unique perspective within the mind, contributing to its complexity. Positioned at C5 on the piano, La Cat resonates as a pivotal note in this mental symphony, representing the realm of love and loneliness.

5. Sozo World and the Magical Adventures:

- Sozo World metaphorically mirrors the vastness of imagination within the mind.

- Attractions like Merfish Loops and Muddlefly Fish Water-Slides represent diverse experiences and emotions encountered within the mind's enchanted landscape. The merfish, now positioned at F5 on the piano, add a unique tonal quality to this whimsical composition.

6. The Glass Piano and the Sea Scale:
   - The glass piano and the "Sea" Scale symbolize the delicate and intercon-
nected nature of the mind.
   - The Sea Scale opens a passage to deeper emotions and thoughts, akin to
the mysteries hidden beneath the surface of the sea in the mind.

7. Realm of Gifts: DeeFlutter and Allace - Gifts of Emotional Connection and
Manipulating Water (People):
   - DeeFlutter's emotional connection ability reflects the depth of understanding within true friendships.
   - Allace, the merfish, utilizes mankind to influence people, symbolizing the
impact of external factors on our emotions and thoughts.
   - Le' Cat's loneliness becomes a metaphor for the emotional complexities
individuals may experience, emphasizing the importance of support and
acceptance.

8. Le' Cat's Chant - Self-Acceptance:
   - Le' Cat's chant, "My name is Nigel Miguel Valentine Revell...but you can
call me Le' Cat," symbolizes self-acceptance and embracing one's true identity
within the symphony of the mind.

Historical Context:

In the context of historical understanding, these characters symbolize vibrations and express archetypes based on the effects of sound. The chromatic
scales, represented by the characters, reflect the vibrational frequencies that
resonate within the mind, influencing thoughts and emotions. The piano
keys they are positioned on signify the specific frequencies at which they
operate, contributing to the overall harmonic composition of the mental
symphony. The historical significance lies in recognizing The Tree of Lives as
a metaphorical setting where the understanding of vibrations and their effects

on the mind was explored, offering a unique perspective on the intersection of music, symbolism, and human psychology.

Comparisons between Sarah from the biblical narrative in Vayera and Le' Cat from the previous imaginative story:

1. Laughter as a Response:
   -Sarah: In Genesis 18:12, Sarah laughs upon hearing the prediction of her bearing a child in her old age. Her laughter is one of disbelief, expressing her skepticism about the possibility.
   -Le' Cat: In the imaginative story, Le' Cat uses laughter to entertain and bring joy. His laughter hides his loneliness, contrasting Sarah's laughter of disbelief.

2. Concealing Emotions:
   -Sarah: Her laughter hides her initial doubt and incredulity. The laughter is a way of concealing her true feelings.
   -Le' Cat: conceals his loneliness behind a façade of adventures masking his emotional struggles.

3. Interaction with Others:
   -Sarah: Interacts with the three divine visitors (angels) with a mix of hospitality and skepticism. Her relationship with Abraham is also tested through the challenges they face.
   -Le' Cat:Interacts with Allace and DeeFlutter and the black elephant in the magical Providence of Sugar Land.

4. Testing Faith and Trust:
   -Sarah: Faces a test of faith in believing that she will conceive in her old age.
   -Le' Cat: Faces moments of doubt and loneliness but ultimately finds trust and friendship with Allace and DeeFlutter. The narrative includes a test of Le' Cat's emotional resilience.

5. Transformation:

   -Sarah: Experiences a transformative moment in her life through the divine promise of a child.

   -Le' Cat: Symbolizes transformation through his shape-shifting abilities. His ability to change appearances reflects adaptability and resilience.

While the contexts are different, exploring these comparisons allows us to draw parallels between the characters' experiences with laughter, concealed emotions, interactions, tests of faith, and transformation in their respective stories.

23

Hypothesis: Le' Cat and Bastet as Sound Archetypes

Remember in **La Cat's Torah portion** Sarah laughed at the thought of becoming pregnant. In the case of La'Cat his pregnancy could be the ability to become a shape shifter. The pregnancy of purpose that he had not mastered yet.Exploring the Harmonic Connections: Le' Cat and Bastet as Sound Archetypes

Drawing insights from the narrative of Le' Cat and the alternative hypothesis for Bastet, we uncover a fascinating hypothetical connection between these two sound archetypes:

1. Protectors and Guides:
   - Le' Cat: Guides in the mystical Province of Sugar Land, offering laughter, joy, and transformation. Implies a protective and guiding role within the realm of sound.
   - Bastet: Protector of lower Egypt, Bastet guides through various aspects, including music. Exhibits protective attributes, mirroring Le' Cat's role as a guardian in the realm of sound.

2. Symbolism of Flexibility and Adaptability:

- Le' Cat: Symbolizes sound's adaptability through shape-shifting abilities. Mirrors sound's capacity to take various forms and adapt to diverse emotional contexts.

- Bastet: Associated with the sun, war, fertility, music, and celebration, suggesting a versatile spectrum of sounds and emotions. Aligns with the adaptability of sound in different cultural and ceremonial contexts.

3. Emphasis on Joyful Sound and Celebration:

- Le' Cat: Associated with laughter, delight, and enchanting experiences, accentuating the positive and uplifting qualities of sound.

- Bastet: Linked to celebrations and festivals, Bastet symbolizes the joyous aspects of sound. Festivals involving raucous celebrations and intoxication align with sound as a source of joy and revelry.

4. Symbolism in Personal Worship:

- Le' Cat: Represents an archetype in the personal sound journeys of individuals. The emotional impact includes both joy and moments of loneliness, akin to the multifaceted nature of sound.

- Bastet: Revered for protection against disease, theft, and as a household guardian. Bastet's role in personal worship involves invoking sound for safety and well-being. The use of cat amulets and special Bast amulets with kittens for fertility suggests a belief in the power of sound healing in various aspects of life.

5. Symbolic Pregnancy of Purpose:

- Le' Cat: Le' Cat's transformative abilities, likened to a pregnancy of purpose, reflect the ongoing journey of self-discovery. The mastery of shape-shifting could symbolize the evolving purpose within the realm of sound.

- Bastet: In the context of sound healing, the protective role of Bastet may be associated with a symbolic pregnancy of purpose, representing the nurturing and growth inherent in sound's healing qualities. The fertility symbolism could extend to the fruitful impact of harmonious sound.

6. Parallel with Sarah's Laughter:

   - Le' Cat: Mirrors Sarah's laughter in the Torah portion. Le' Cat's laughter and moments of loneliness may echo the complexities and paradoxes within the emotional spectrum associated with sound.

   - Bastet: The laughter and joyous celebrations associated with Bastet may parallel Sarah's laughter. Both signify the multifaceted nature of human emotions and their connection to sound and celebration.

This exploration suggests a harmonious resonance between Le' Cat and Bastet as sound archetypes, weaving protective, versatile, and emotionally rich narratives within the vast tapestry of sound and its impact on human experience.

About the Author

Tashlultum Levy is an author and visionary explorer whose literary journey transcends the ordinary boundaries of fiction. Born with a passion for unraveling the mysteries of sound and the cosmic symphony, Tashlultum has dedicated her creative endeavors to crafting narratives that blend the fantastical with the profound.

Guided by a divine revelation, Levy has embraced an unusual assignment, becoming a custodian of an ancient child, Tashlultum, the Queen of Sound. This metamorphosis, much like the evolution of Sari into Sarah, symbolizes a transformative journey aligned with the role that God intended.

Drawing inspiration from the echoes of epochs long past, levy navigates the corridors of time, seeking to leave a resonant legacy for future generations. The intricacies of Tashlultum's sonic sovereignty unfold under her pen, weaving a tapestry of sound and wisdom that transcends the boundaries of time and space.

In addition to her role as an author, Levy is a seeker of enlightenment, finding profound meaning in the interplay of pain and enlightenment. This duality is reflected not only in her narrative but also in her acknowledgment of those who brought pain, recognizing the transformative power inherent in life's challenges.

Levy's work stands as a testament to the enduring power of sound and its ability to resonate through generations. Through the exploration of celestial muses and the harmonies interwoven into the fabric of existence, her invites readers on a journey of self-discovery, spiritual awakening, and the extraordinary possibilities that lie within the ordinary.

As a custodian of ancient secrets and a guardian of sonic sovereignty, levy invites readers to explore the depths of their potential, harmonizing with the frequencies of their existence, and becoming a part of the eternal tapestry of sound and wisdom.